(And How We Got It Wrong)

Salvation
(And How We Got It Wrong)

by

Kenneth N. Myers

Mayeux Press
DENISON, TEXAS

Salvation (And How We Got It Wrong)

© Copyright 2013 by Kenneth N. Myers
All rights reserved
This book or parts thereof may not be reproduced in any form, stored in a retrieval system, or transmitted in any form by any means - electronic, mechanical, photocopy, recording or otherwise - without prior written permission of the publisher, except as provided by United States of America copyright law.

Unless otherwise indicated, Scripture quotations are from The Holy Bible, English Standard Version® (ESV®), copyright © 2001 by Crossway, a publishing ministry of Good News Publishers. Used by permission. All rights reserved.

Myers, Kenneth Neal, 1959-
Salvation (And How We Got It Wrong)/Kenneth N. Myers

1. Soteriology   2. Christian Theology

Cover design: Neal Mayeux
The Crucifixion by Gustave Doré

Published by Mayeux Press
561 Bailey Drive, Denison TX 75091

To the motley crew at r/christianity

silouan
funny_original_name
partofaplan
namer98
Jo_Nah
p1k4chu
US_Hiker
Average560
Kidnapped_David_Bal4
gingerkid1234
BranchDavidian
Aceofspades25
WC_Cowpony
Irondog 1970
thephotoman
KSW1

Acknowledgements

Thank you to the clergy and people of Church of the Resurrection, Sherman, Texas, who have faithfully stood with me in the ministry of teaching.

Thank you to Pastor Josh Burton who helped me bounce around ideas about this book.

Thank you to Scott Rudy for editing, proofreading, and suggestions.

Thank you to my wife Shirley who is unflagging in her support.

Thank you to Tom at *Hotel Luz en Yucatan*, Merida, Mexico, who provided a peaceful haven for writing.

Table of Contents

Foreword		11
Chapter 1	Jesus Paid It All	17
Chapter 2	Where The Story Came From	35
Chapter 3	Original Sin	53
Chapter 4	*Cur Deus Homo*	61
Chapter 5	Propitiation and Sacrifice	89
Chapter 6	The Process Of Being Saved	113

Foreword

This is a very small book about a very big subject. Salvation is at the very center (shall we say, at the very foundation) of Christian thinking. The subject of salvation (soteriology for you who prefer the fancy theological term) asks all the profound questions. Since they are deep questions, instead of just reading through this list, pause a moment and consider each question and at least briefly ask yourself to answer them:

• What does salvation even *mean*?

• What do we need to be saved *from*, and (almost never asked in our Western, Evangelical Christian way of thinking), what are we being saved *to*?

- What is sin? Does it really matter? Is it personal? Is it inherited? Is it even my fault?

- What did Jesus actually accomplish on the cross? *Why* did Jesus have to die?

- What is the role of God the Father in our salvation?

Christians have been working hard to answer these questions for centuries - no, for millennia. And the answers we have come up with have often been very different from each other. The early Church Fathers tackled the big questions and answered them for their own generations, with their own insights. Later generations would see new twists to the questions and find new answers in response. Whole theological systems would develop, over the course of centuries, attempting to give solid, historic, biblical, practical, applicable answers to the questions being asked.

A lot of the time the answers were flavored or influenced by the culture in which the thinkers were thinking and the writers were writing. Without question this volume also is influenced by the culture in which I am thinking and writing - but this is also the culture I am attempting to speak to, to help, because I am convinced we have bought into an understanding of salvation that is *taken as a given* to be biblical and true, and yet when closely considered simply doesn't hold up to scrutiny. I know many people who have ultimately rejected Christianity partially and significantly because of the answers they have received to these big questions. Closely inspected, the answers simply didn't make sense. They weren't well thought out, but were simply parroted from what had come before, and ultimately were inadequate in dealing with the questions.

Another Small Book

This is a very short book, only 121 pages long. But a thousand years ago another very short book (only 98 pages in the English translation) hit the Western Christian world and left a significant impact on how we think about and answer the salvation questions. Anselm, the Archbishop of Canterbury, England (though an Italian by birth and training) wrote *Cur Deus Homo*, or, as we know it in English, *Why God Became Man*. 98 pages, but it influenced generations - centuries - a millennium - of Christians, right down to, almost certainly, *you*.

And I will argue here that Anselm (and the Reformers who followed him) simply got it wrong.

How dare I suggest such a thing? How can I, in my ridiculously limited and insufficient wisdom and understanding, even think to disagree with such luminaries of Christian thought? Can I possibly pit myself against these intellectual and theological giants and even hope to show them flawed? Of course, I cannot, in my own simple way of thinking, hope to stand *contra* these luminaries. But maybe - just perhaps - I can stand on the shoulders of giants who came before them and point to a way of thinking about salvation that will be biblical and make good sense.

And maybe - just perhaps - in looking at fresh (yet very old) answers, I can also help people change their understanding not only of salvation, but also of God himself.

I hope by the end of this small book you will be convinced in your mind, and especially in your heart, that what Saint John wrote (in 1 John 4.8) is really, unequivocally true: "God is love." God *is* love, God loves *you*, God loves *everyone*, and there is *no part of God* that doesn't love you!

Though I am about to disagree strongly with Anselm, I can agree completely with the opening of his book, and I wish to mimic his spirit in my own writing:

> "But my attempt will take the form not so much of a demonstration as of an enquiry undertaken jointly with you, and it will be made with the stipulation which I wish to be understood to apply to all that I say, namely, that if I say something which is not confirmed by a source of greater authority - even if I seem to be proving it by means of logic - it is to be accepted with only this degree of certainty: that it seems to be so provisionally, until God shall in some way reveal to me something better. If, moreover, it comes about that I seem to any extent to be replying satisfactorily to your question, it ought to be regarded as a certainty that someone wiser than I could to this more fully. Indeed, it is a matter of certain knowledge that, whatever a human being may say on this subject, there remain deeper reasons, as yet hidden from us, for a reality of such supreme

importance." - *Cur Deus Homo*, Book One, Chapter Two.

Chapter One

Jesus Paid It All
The Story We Have Been Told

Dear Bishop Myers:

I'm writing you because I've seen a few things you have had to say about salvation, and I just don't see how it squares with the Bible. It almost seems like you don't think the death of Jesus was even necessary to secure our salvation. I would love to discuss this with you and see if we are saying the same thing in different ways, or if you are saying something completely different. Honestly, I don't even know if what you believe can be considered orthodox Christian belief.

Please write when you have time, and help me work through some of these questions.

Sincerely,

Victor Anselmo Boso

❉ ❉ ❉ ❉ ❉ ❉ ❉ ❉ ❉ ❉ ❉ ❉ ❉ ❉ ❉ ❉ ❉ ❉

Dear Victor:

Thank you for writing to me, and for asking me for further details rather than just simply dismissing me and assuming things about me. Sometimes it is very frustrating when people *think* they know my position on some matter, then go tell others what I believe, and get it completely wrong! Let me begin by assuring you that I am indeed orthodox in my understanding of salvation - in fact I have a personal commitment to not believe *anything* not taught by faithful teachers in the early church era.

But if we are going to have a decent conversation about these things, maybe the first thing is for you to explain to me your own understanding of salvation: what happens, why it happens and how it happens. I'll be looking forward to hearing from you soon.

God bless you,

Bishop Ken

P.S. If you don't mind, tell me a little about you - it's nice to know who I'm conversing with!

❋❋❋❋❋❋❋❋❋❋❋❋❋❋❋❋❋❋❋

Dear Ken (may I call you Ken? You signed off your last letter with your first name):

> *I am Victor Anselmo Boso, I'm 35 years old and single. My parents are Italian, but I was born in Switzerland and we moved to the United States when I was fifteen. I have had a rather circuitous spiritual journey - I was baptized in the Catholic Church, but never really had much of a faith as a child. My parents didn't raise me faithfully in the church - we only attended for Easter and Christmas and a few other occasions, like weddings or funerals. When I was in high school I got saved in an Evangelical church. For the next ten years or so I found myself growing in the Lord, but also moving around a lot, looking for deeper*

experiences in the Lord and greater understanding of the Word of God. I spent a lot of time in a Pentecostal/Charismatic church, then got involved in a pretty conservative Presbyterian church where I learned about John Calvin and his teachings. After a few years there I kind of settled into a middle-of-the-road non-denominational church that focused on solid Bible teaching without too much emphasis on specific doctrinal stands.

But, in all my spiritual journeying, it seems to me that every church I can remember being a part of pretty much said the same thing about salvation. Here is a brief rundown of what I believe. I will line it out so you can follow along. Surely you must be familiar with this, although it seems to me you don't believe it (or at least not all of it), and that is what puzzles me so much.

God Made Humans And All Was Good

First, God created humanity in a state of moral and spiritual perfection. There was no sin in the world, and no death. Things were good - in fact God called it "very good." God put the first humans, Adam and Eve, in a garden paradise where they had everything they could possibly need, and most importantly they had God himself. There was only one rule for them to follow: "Do not eat from the tree of the knowledge of good and evil." God also told them what the punishment would be if they broke the rule - "but of the tree of the knowledge of good and evil you shall not eat, for in the day that you eat of it you shall surely die" (Genesis 2.17).

Humans Sinned And God Cursed Them

But of course (obviously you already know this) they did *eat from that tree. Eve was tempted by the Devil to eat the fruit so she could "be like God." She ate, and so did Adam, and as a result God cursed them. He had told them that he would punish them if they ate from the tree, and when they broke his commandment, he kept his word. They died. Maybe not that very moment, but they were cast out of the Garden of Eden, had to fend for themselves in the wilderness world, had to work hard just to stay alive, and ultimately they died.*

Everyone Is Born A Sinner Under God's Judgment

Ever since Adam and Eve, every descendant of theirs - every person who has ever lived - has been born a sinner, and is therefore automatically under the wrath of God. From the time of our conception, no one escapes this sinful nature. It is in our DNA. We can't help it, and we are helpless to repair the damage done. Paul wrote, "Therefore, just as sin came into the world through one man, and death through sin, and so death spread to all men because all sinned..." (Romans 5.12).

So, the situation of every person is that they are conceived and born as, so to speak, enemies of God, and they are helpless to change this in their own powers. They aren't good enough. They are sinful. God cannot have fellowship with sinful humanity, and the unavoidable consequence of the fact of their very existence is eternal condemnation. They can't save themselves, so they need a savior.

Jesus Christ Is The Great Substitute

Because humanity is sinful, and therefore under the just wrath of God, God sent his Son to be born as a human being, born of a Virgin, sharing in our humanity, "one who in every respect has been tempted as we are, yet without sin" (Hebrews 4.15). Jesus lived a perfect, sinless life, but he died a sinner's death. So, he became our substitute, and he paid God for our debt of sin. So now, anyone who puts their trust in his work - in his payment - receives forgiveness through him.

Let me say it like this: Jesus, being sinless, did not deserve death. We, being sinful, deserve nothing but death. On the cross there was a great exchange, and Jesus substituted himself for us. When I was a teenager we used to sing a song that captures this in a nutshell -

> *He paid a debt he did not owe,*
> *I owed a debt I could not pay,*
> *I needed someone to wash my sins away...*

In fact, now that I think of it, this is so central to our faith that a lot of our songs address it:

> *Jesus paid it all,*
> *All to him I owe,*
> *Sin had left a crimson stain,*
> *He washed me white as snow.*

When I was in the Pentecostal church we used to sing about it too. I think the song was called The Old Account Was Settled Long Ago:

> *There was a time on earth*
> *When in the book of heaven*
> *An old account was standing*
> *For sins yet unforgiven.*
>
> *My name was at the top*
> *With many things below*
> *I went unto the Keeper*
> *And settled long ago.*

The point being, the only way we can settle the account of our sins is through Jesus and his death on the cross. I can't pay my own debt because I am spiritually bankrupt and I can't even stand before a just God because of my sinfulness. I need someone else to pay the penalty for me, to settle the account.

One more song to make my point, and then I'll get on with this discussion. This one is called He Brought Me Out:

> *My heart was distressed*
> *'Neath Jehovah's dread frown,*
> *And low in the pit*
> *Where my sins dragged me down;*
> *I cried to the Lord from the deep miry clay,*
> *Who tenderly brought me out to golden day.*

Do you see the point of all this? Let me put it plainly and succinctly: Because of my sinful nature (and my actual sins) God is rightfully wrathful. I cannot bear to stand in his perfect presence. He cannot bear to stand in my sinful presence. He cannot forgive me unless the price of my sins is paid. I cannot pay that price. So Jesus pays that price for me, and I am reconciled to God. I am saved! Praise God, because of his mercy, I am saved from eternal damnation and from eternal separation from God.

Now, because I have accepted the payment that Christ made for me, and because I make no pretense of being able to pay for my own sins, when I die I will go to heaven, and not hell, and I will live eternally with God in his glory.

Thank you for enduring this long letter. This, in a nutshell is what I believe. It is what I have been taught. It is, as I understand it, the Gospel, and what all Christians believe. That is why it disturbs me somewhat when I read some of the things you are saying - it seems like you don't agree with this. How can you, as a Christian minister and a person committed to the Word of God, not believe this?

Looking forward to your reply,

Victor Anselmo Boso

P.S. If I may call you Ken, you may call me Andy - it's what all my friends call me.

❈❈❈❈❈❈❈❈❈❈❈❈❈❈❈❈❈

Dear Andy:

First, let's get rid of the formalities. As a boy, my family and friends called me Kenny. As a teenager, it became Ken. As an adult, it became Kenneth. I used to not care for my name, but my favorite figure from church history is the Irish saint Columba. When I learned that his best friend was St. Kenneth, I suddenly took a new liking to my name. Anyway, after ordination it became Father Ken, then Bishop Ken. For the sake of these letters, I'll call you Andy and you call me Ken or Kenneth, whatever suits your fancy.

Thank you for your brief but thorough description of how you understand salvation to work. What you have described is indeed the "standard" (or shall I say, "popular" - because it is most predominant in our part of Christianity) view of salvation. And you are also correct that I don't believe it. I used to. Early on it was the view I grew up with and the only view I knew about. I heard it as a child, learned about it in college and seminary, preached it and believed it. A number of years ago it started to unravel in my mind as I read Scripture more thoroughly and as I read the early Fathers of the Church. The idea simply wasn't around in the beginning, and that troubled me. For several years I kind of kept it on the back burner, knowing it was there and accepting it, but not being comfortable with it. Later, I came to the place of completely rejecting it - perhaps we can discuss that paradigm shift later on.

If you want to use theological terms and phrases, what you have described is the *Theory of Penal Substitutionary Atonement*. We in Evangelical circles tend to accept it not only as *our understanding* of how salvation works, but as actually *the clear biblical truth* of how salvation works. But I would like to point out that it is a "theory," and that any decent theological dictionary (not to mention more focused texts) will list it as one theory among a half dozen or more theories - ways to understand - regarding the Atonement.

I hope you will not simply dismiss me, and end this conversation, just because I admit that I no longer hold to this view, and in fact see the view as actually very *unbiblical*.

But *if* this conversation is to continue, I would like to stall my discussion of the subject for a bit, and ask you some questions to get you thinking about what you actually believe. Please take time to ponder these questions. Don't answer them automatically or in some rote fashion. Think them through. These are some questions that kept popping up in my own mind and giving me trouble.

OK. Here we go. These are not in any particular order, and I promise to address them more thoroughly if you choose to continue this dialogue, but here are some questions for you to consider:

Why Are We Punished For Adam's Sin?

Why should we believe that we are punished for our ancestors' sin? Adam and Eve sinned. But why should their descendants be punished for their sin? Doesn't the Bible clearly say that punishment shouldn't work this way?

> "Fathers shall not be put to death because of their children, nor shall children be put to death because of their fathers. Each one shall be put to death for his own sin" (Deuteronomy 24.16).

> "The soul who sins shall die. The son shall not suffer for the iniquity of the father, nor the father suffer for the iniquity of the son. The righteousness of the righteous shall be upon himself, and

the wickedness of the wicked shall be upon himself" (Ezekiel 18.20).

And yet, we are told that God does this very thing - he curses us, is wrathful toward us, even before we have committed any actual sins. We are conceived and born as just recipients of his wrath because we are heirs of Adam's sin. Seems to me that God instructs us to behave in one way, while he behaves in a different way. It doesn't make a lick of sense to me.

Why Can't God Just Forgive Us?

The *Theory of Penal Substitutionary Atonement* (I'll call it PSA) says that in order to obtain forgiveness, a payment for our sins has to be made. But is this at all what the Bible teaches us about how forgiveness works? I mean, honestly, if *we* applied this rule to our forgiving, would it at all be in keeping with the teachings of Jesus about how we are to forgive? "When you forgive, first make sure that the offending party pays up!" Can you imagine Jesus saying anything like this? If we are taught by God to forgive without payment, then why doesn't God do the same?

Is Justice Served With The Punishment of the Innocent?

PSA teaches that we couldn't pay for our own sins, so an innocent person had to die for us. But is that really justice? If someone commits a crime against you, and gets caught, but can't make restitution, would you consider it just and fair and right to say, "Well, OK - but *someone* has to pay before I forgive" - and then you find some completely innocent person and make them pay up - even if their action is voluntary? Restitution may have been made, but has justice really been served?

What Does Justice Even Mean?

I think we throw the term *justice* around a bit too loosely. Justice, ultimately, means setting things right. If a wicked man murders someone's daughter, he may go to prison for the rest of his life, or he may even suffer capital punishment, and we say, "Justice has been served," but really it hasn't. The only way the thing can actually be "made right" is for the daughter to be given back her life.

With PSA, we say that humans are wickedly sinful, and have offended against God's honor and righteousness, and that justice must be served, so Jesus dies on our behalf. But does that really *fix* anything? How does Jesus, the innocent victim dying to *pay* for our sins, bring about a "setting things right"? I mean, even if we were to die for our own sins, and be eternally condemned to hell, how does that "set things right"? How does that give back to God the honor we have stolen from him?

Is There One God And Is He Schizophrenic?

The cornerstone of Christian truth is that there is one God. Not thousands, not dozens, not three - One God. When Jesus was asked what is the greatest commandment, he answered by quoting Deuteronomy 6.4: "Hear O Israel, the Lord our God, the Lord is one." Whatever else Christians believe, we believe that there is one God. That one God is revealed to us as Father, Son and Holy Spirit, but God isn't some kind of committee of divine beings.

PSA, it seems to me, juxtaposes the Father against the Son. The Father is the wrathful and just God who demands payment for our sins (although he teaches us to forgive others without payment). The Son is the loving God who says, in effect, "Father - I will go and pay for the sins of humanity. I will become a perfect, sinless human, and you can pour out your wrath on me instead of them, and that will satisfy your justice." By the way, *satisfaction* is an important word in PSA. The Father demands satisfaction, but can't find it in all of humanity ("I can't get no satisfaction" - to quote that illustrious theologian Mick Jagger), so the Son offers to satisfy the Father's demand of payment by sacrificing himself.

But doesn't our salvation originate in the very heart of the Father? The most famous verse in the whole Bible is John 3.16: "For God so loved the world, that he gave his only Son, that whoever believes in him should not perish but have eternal life." *The Father* so loved the world! This doesn't sound like a wrathful God demanding satisfaction, it sounds like a loving God planning a rescue for those he loves.

You don't have to answer this letter in a hurry. Take your time, think through the questions, and write back after you've had some time to really contemplate these questions.

Ken

❈ ❈ ❈ ❈ ❈ ❈ ❈ ❈ ❈ ❈ ❈ ❈ ❈ ❈ ❈ ❈ ❈ ❈ ❈

Kenneth:

Wow! You've asked some very good questions, and I promise you I will think long and hard about them. Even just a brief reading over the questions makes me see some difficulties with, as you call it, "the theory" of salvation that I have understood.

I will give these questions more thought, but something you said made me curious. You said, "The idea simply wasn't around in the beginning." Well, if it wasn't around in the beginning, then where did it come from? I just assumed this is what all Christians in all times have believed. You are right - I haven't seen this as one theory among many regarding how we are saved, I have just assumed it was the biblical truth. While I think about these questions, would you mind lining out for me where this idea came from and how it became so prevalent?

Anxiously awaiting your reply,

Andy

Chapter Two

Where The Story Came From
Skip this chapter if you hate history!

Dear Andy:

In your last letter you seemed surprised that the *Theory of Penal Substitutionary Atonement* wasn't the universal understanding of how we are saved, and you asked me where the idea came from.

I don't know how much of a history buff you are, so I won't write an entire tome on the history of the development of this doctrine, but please allow me to sketch a brief overview of how it came about.

First, let me make it clear that it didn't just "pop up" overnight. It developed, one piece at a time, over the course of more than a thousand years.

As I said before, the idea of PSA simply didn't exist in the early centuries of Christianity. In fact, it didn't exist as a the full blown theory that we know about until the Sixteenth Century! Although seeds of the theory were sown in the Fourth Century, *the Church didn't have this notion for fifteen hundred years*! In other words, on the grand scale of history, PSA is a relatively recent development. For the sake of simplicity (again, I don't know how *into* doctrinal history you are), I will break down the development into three pieces.

Augustine and Original Sin

I don't know if you know anything about Saint Augustine but the man was a genius, and his thoughts have been formative in Western Christianity, since, well, since he wrote and ministered in the Fourth and Fifth Centuries. So much of which followed in the Christian West was built upon his theology, and I think it is safe to say that, beyond Jesus and Saint Paul, Augustine becomes foundational to the development of doctrine in the West. So, humor me for a bit and let me tell you about him then I would like to tell you about one of his doctrines in particular, the doctrine of Original Sin.

Augustine was born in 354 in what is now Algeria. Just to put things in perspective, his country was part of the Roman Empire which circled the Mediterranean Sea, and he was born a quarter century *after* the first great Ecumenical Council in Nicaea (from which we get the Nicene Creed). His father was a pagan and his mother a Christian, and he was raised up as a Christian but as a young man got involved in a cult that basically celebrated debauchery. As a young man he had an ongoing affair with a woman who bore him a son, and during his wild days he prayed his now famous prayer, "God grant me chastity...but not yet!" Augustine converted to Christianity in 386, at the age of of 32, and was baptized a year later in the Italian city of Milan. Ten years later he became the bishop of Hippo (again, think Algeria). But what happened *before* his conversion is what I would like to point out now.

Augustine was trained in classical rhetoric. Now, today when we use the word rhetoric we think of logic and argument and making a good case for something, but the field that rhetoric originally took root in was politics and law. So, to put it simplistically, Augustine was trained as a lawyer. After his conversion his training in rhetoric would serve him well as he applied it to theology, but what is important to see is that Western (and particularly Augustinian) theology tends to be rooted in the legal. It almost unavoidably approaches things from a legal standpoint. Christians in the East thought and wrote from a more holistic, less legal framework, but the Roman world was a world of legal thinking. Rome itself, as the center of the Empire, was obviously, culturally, a city given to legal thinking, and this dramatically affected the emerging doctrines of the West.

As I have said, Augustine was a genius, and he wrote many wonderful commentaries on the Scriptures, hundreds of letters, and whole books of theological reasoning based on his training as a rhetorician. His school of thought continued (and continues even today) to influence Western Christianity, and so it is only natural to see Western theology emerge with a strong focus on the legal side of things. Coincidentally, more than a thousand years later, another trained lawyer, John Calvin, would take Augustine's ideas and expand them into an even more developed legal framework.

One of the doctrines developed by Augustine, which would completely saturate Western thinking, was the doctrine of *Original Sin*. Although a few earlier Fathers discussed it in rather ambiguous terms (Irenaeus, for example), Augustine was the one who gave it wings to fly.

He taught that Adam's sin (the *original* sin) was transmitted to all his descendants. Through the very act of sexual reproduction, we are all conceived and born, not only with an *inclination* to sin, but as already *condemned* because of sinful nature. To Augustine (and those who would follow in his tracks for centuries to come), every human is born not only with the *tendency* to sin, but also under the *guilt* of sin. We are born hell bound. Only baptism would take away this guilt, and anyone who had the misfortune of not being baptized was ultimately headed to eternity without God. So, even someone who died in infancy, before committing a single actual sin, unless baptized, would go to hell (or at best, to a kind of "upper level" of hell called Limbo, where they wouldn't really suffer much, but could never, for all eternity, have the joy of knowing and seeing God). While the Western Church never fully and officially endorsed

Augustine's view, it most definitely had a near universal impact on Western theology.

The thing I would have you note here, however, is the legal framework of the doctrine. In practice it became very *transactional*. You are a sinner, bound for hell. You get baptized. Through the grace of baptism you are forgiven, washed clean of original sin, and you are moved over from the condemned column to the being-saved column.

Anselm And The Doctrine Of Satisfaction

Things hummed along nicely after Augustine for a half a millennium or so until Anselm of Canterbury shows up on the scene (I'm assuming, whether you realize it or not, that you are probably indirectly named after him). Anselm was the Archbishop of Canterbury in the Eleventh Century. Now, when people think about the ABC (Archbishop of Canterbury) they think, quite rightly, of England and the Church of England. But this is five hundred years before the Church of England parted ways with the Church of Rome, and Anselm actually wasn't English, he was Italian.

For what it's worth (and it's worth something), Anselm's father was a very abusive man. Just keep that in mind.

Transferred from Italy to France and finally to England, the good and godly Anselm assumed leadership of the English church (very reluctantly, I might add) in 1093. He was exiled twice from England, and wrote many significant works of theology, but the one for which he will forevermore be remembered was *Cur Deus Homo - Why God Became Man*.

It was a tiny book, but it had a major impact on Western Christianity. The English translation is only 98 pages, but its influence changed the course of theology in the West forever, especially when the Reformers expanded its ideas (but more about that later). In *Cur Deus Homo*, Anselm laid out a theory of the Atonement based on the offended honor of God. Taking his cue from the medieval notions of the honor of kings (and perhaps the psychological pain of an abusive father?), Anselm argued that, in disobeying God, Adam offended the honor of the Creator and King of all things. The only way for that honor to be restored was for punishment to be meted out, and this case, since the honor was ultimate and the thus the dishonor was ultimate, the ultimate price had to be paid - death.

Running forward with Augustine's notion of Original Sin - that we were all "in Adam" when he sinned, and consequently humanity at large is a *massa damnata* (a damned mass, a condemned group - Augustine's words, not Anselm's), we were all - both singularly and collectively - completely unable to restore the honor that had been stolen.

If you steal from someone, it is not enough to give back what you have stolen - their honor has still been offended, they have still suffered angst and harm even if their goods have been returned. So even if Adam (and all the rest of us) could somehow make up for our sins, that is not enough, it doesn't balance the scales. God has still been dishonored. Anselm said it like this:

"If an angel or a man were always to render to God what he owes, he would never sin." He goes on, "Then, to sin is nothing other than not to give God what is owed to him." Got it? But man *did* sin. So, "Someone who does not render to God this honor due to him is taking away from God what is his, and dishonoring God, and this is what it is to sin.

As long as he does not repay what he has taken away, he remains in a state of guilt. And it is not sufficient merely to repay what has been taken away: rather, he ought to pay back more than he took...Therefore, everyone who sins is under an obligation to repay to God the honor which he has violently taken from him, and this is the satisfaction which every sinner is obliged to give to God" (Book One, Chapter 11).

We can't even pay God back for the sins we have committed, let alone go the additional step and pay "extra" for his damaged honor. So, Anselm concludes, "Therefore, it is not fitting for God to forgive a sin without punishment" (1.12).

Anselm goes on to say that God created man to replace the fallen angels of heaven, and, "It is not fitting, then, for God to receive into heaven, for the replacement of the fallen angels, a human sinner who has not paid recompense" (1.19). He spends pages arguing that God simply *cannot* forgive us our sins without punishment. Our punishment is death and hell, but even if we suffer death and hell to the fullest, we can't make up for the dishonor we have brought to God. We are, as we say in Texas, up a creek without a paddle.

No, we're up a creek without a boat. We may even be up a creek without a creek!

What Anselm says makes a certain logical sense, but I would (and will) argue that it is built on a faulty foundation - a foundation of medieval kings, and not the revelation of the nature of God in the Scriptures. Are you tracking so far? I know it's a little complicated, but keep going with me.

In Book Two (the second section of the short *Cur Deus Homo*), Anselm goes on to say that, since a man (or all humanity) committed the egregious acts of dishonor, it is only a man (representing all of mankind) who can pay the debt owed. But no man is even *able* to pay, because, since we owe a perfect life to God, and since all of us have sinned, none of us can pay what is owed. Satisfaction must be made to the King, but this is impossible to do. So, God becomes man in the person of Christ, and as a man, living a perfect life, pays the debt. He suffers an undeserved death in order to balance the books, to restore the honor of God, and to reconcile humanity to the offended God. "Christ of his own accord gave to his Father what he was never going to lose as a matter of necessity, and he paid, on behalf of sinners, a debt which he did not owe" (2.18).

And *there*, Andy, is the soil from which those songs you mentioned in an earlier letter spring up. The whole idea of Jesus *paying* the Father finds its first flowering in Anselm of Canterbury. In his own time, and later, there were many other theologians in the West who disagreed with him, but Anselm's thinking won the day and influenced Western Christianity in a major way.

John Calvin And The Reformers

This is the last bit of history, I promise! I hope you have hung with me this far and haven't given up the ghost. The final piece jumps forward another five hundred years from Anselm, to the Sixteenth Century, which was what we would call "a sea change" in the life of Europe and Western Christianity. I'm sure you already know, at least in a cursory way, the story of the Reformation. Luther in Germany, the 95 Theses, the Anglican severance from Rome, John Calvin in Switzerland - the whole of Europe was in political and religious upheaval, society was being turned head on heels, and chaos was the order of the day. The Church of Rome was watching its influence shatter, new churches and new nations were emerging on the left and on the right, and theology, at least on some level, was breaking forth with new ideas and insights.

John Calvin was a Swiss - get this - lawyer! Here is not the place to look at all of Calvin's insights and innovations, but we need to focus on one major transition that he and several of the other Reformers made. They all pretty much accepted the by-then-standard Anselmian notion of Satisfaction. But when Anselm wrote five hundred years before, the offended entity was the king. A crime against any in the land was a crime against the king, because he ruled everyone and everything in the land. To this day in lands that have a monarchy, the trial is usually stated as, "The Queen vs. John Doe". Now, with the various monarchies tending to lose their power if not their heads, the focus turned from the king to the court, the trials became "The State vs. John Doe". So, when Calvin and the Reformers expanded on Anselm's teaching they took it out of the realm of the kings and placed it in the realm of the judges. God became man, yes, to pay for our sins, but as Calvin stylized it, mankind stood before God the righteous *Judge*, and Jesus was "made a substitute and a surety in the place of transgressors and even submitted as a criminal, to sustain and suffer all the punishment which would have been inflicted on them" (Calvin's *Institutes*, 2.16.10).

With the Reformers, Anselm's doctrine of *Substitution* became the Doctrine of Penal Substitutionary Atonement. It was no longer about the honor of a king being offended, it was about a crime against God, he himself being the righteous Judge, meting out the penalty of death and eternal damnation to all sinners (which is all of us). Christ came, it was argued, to pay the just penalty for our sins, in order to save us from it. Anselm's *debt* becomes the Reformer's *penalty*. Penal (a penalty must be paid) Substitutionary (by someone else because we can't pay it ourselves) Atonement (in order to reconcile us to God).

And so, within the Evangelical world today (whether that be Evangelical Baptists or Methodists or Anglicans or Pentecostals or whatever else), the doctrine of PSA has become the *ipso facto* doctrine of the Atonement - of *why* Christ died for us.

PSA - Foreign To The East

Andy, do you know anything about the Eastern Orthodox Church? Most Western Christians don't. A lot know nothing *at all* about it and when you mention it look at you with curiosity and say something like, "Orthodox - isn't that *Jewish*?" And I must say that the Orthodox Church is indeed foreign to most of us because it is...well...*Eastern*, and we are Western. We live in the Western World, we think like the Western World, we are products of the Western World, we are part of the Western World. East is East and West is West and never the twain shall meet!

However, if I mention some particular congregations in the Eastern Orthodox Church you will recognize them immediately. Let's try it: Antioch, Ephesus, Philippi, Corinth, Smyrna, Athens. Sure you have heard of them - anyone who reads their Bible has heard of them! The startling thing is, these churches still exist, and they are all Eastern Orthodox. Here is not the place to go into the history of Orthodoxy (aren't you glad?), but suffice it to say that, while the Western Church grew in Europe, and later in Australia and North and South America and other places impacted by the European conquests, the Eastern Church continued to grow in Northern Africa, Asia Minor, the Middle East, Eastern Europe and parts of Asia.

The East was separated from the West geographically, politically, and theologically, and in 1054 something called "The Great Schism" happened which divided the Church in a terrible way. Our prayers are that God will someday reunite us, but it is important for us to recognize that Christianity has continued in the East just as it has in the West.

Why am I bringing this up? Because I find it significant that the various developments we've been talking about - Augustine's *Original Sin*, Anselm's *Satisfaction*, and the Reformer's *Penal Substitutionary Atonement* are completely foreign to Eastern Christianity. It simply isn't on their map; it has never been a part of their theology or way of thinking.

This fact in itself is no arbiter of the truth or falsehood of a particular doctrine, but think about it - if a particular doctrine were simply "biblical," wouldn't it be found first of all, in the ancient Church, and secondly, in the *whole* Church? For example, core doctrines such as the divinity of Christ, the Holy Trinity, the Virgin Birth, the Resurrection of Jesus, the promise of the Second Coming - all of these are held by all Christians as essentials of the faith, and yet, here is a doctrinal development that is completely foreign to an entire, ancient, doctrinally solid, venerable part of the Church! We can argue about the merits (or lack thereof) of the doctrine, but can we really argue for its essentiality? And yet, for so many Christians, particularly in the Evangelical world, we just take for granted that PSA is the only doctrine of the Atonement out there, and if someone doesn't believe it we look at them as possibly heretical!

Thank you, my friend, for enduring this long lesson in the history of theological development. The short version is this: Augustine's doctrine of *Original Sin* blossomed into Anselm's doctrine of *Satisfaction* which fully flowered into the Reformers' doctrine of *Penal Substitutionary Atonement* which so permeated the Evangelical world that it is by and large accepted as the *only* doctrine of the Atonement out there. And I am convinced it is completely wrong.

I know that was a lot to take take in, and I hope it didn't throw our conversation off track. Write back if you have a mind to.

God bless you,

Kenneth

❊ ❊ ❊ ❊ ❊ ❊ ❊ ❊ ❊ ❊ ❊ ❊ ❊ ❊ ❊ ❊ ❊ ❊

Dear Ken:

Oh my goodness! I had no idea that my doctrine of salvation had such a complex history! Thank you for taking time to spell it out for me. It is indeed a lot to take in, and I'm going to be mulling over it, but I see now that what I thought was just a given, a Gospel truth, isn't quite as "given" as I thought it was! I've also had a little time to think over the questions you posed in your previous letter, and I must admit that they unsettled me a bit.

I fear that my response will be rather brief compared to your long letter. But here is my question: if PSA isn't the way to believe, then please do share with me what you think is the right belief. If you don't mind, start with that whole Original Sin thing because, although I haven't studied it much, I have just accepted that the doctrine of Original Sin was a doctrine accepted by all Christians. If you don't agree with Augustine, then just what do *you think?*

Oh - and I had no idea that I was indirectly named after Saint Anselm!

Andy - Victor ANSELMO Boso

Chapter Three

Original Sin

Dear Andy:

In the last letter you requested that, if I don't believe in *Penal Substitutionary Atonement* would I please tell you what I do believe, and you asked me to start with the subject of original sin. That seems to me to be a good place to begin, so let's have at it.

Briefly (and thus, perhaps, somewhat lacking in necessary nuances), the West (Rome, and her children, the Protestants, who quickly threw off *much* that was Roman but held fiercely and even intensified her soteriology) sees original sin as something that affects the very *nature* of humanity.

Do you use, or have, a *New International Version* of the Bible? As a translation it gives a good example of what I'm talking about. In the 1984 edition (thankfully they changed it in later editions) 22 times they translate Paul's use of the word *sarx* as "sinful nature". Now, the word *sarx* means "flesh," and is one of Paul's theological terms, but it *doesn't* mean "sinful nature" (there are Greek words for "sinful" and for "nature" and none of them have anything to do with the word *sarx*). But the translation shows how Evangelical Christians tend to *think* about the whole issue. We are born (nay, conceived), in the very make up of our being, in a state of sinfulness and estrangement from God. As I pointed out to you in the letter about history, Augustine, and of course Calvin after him, had a field day with this notion.

The Eastern (and earlier patristic) view is that sin has crept in as a kind of spiritual disease, which is manifest in particular sins - in thought, word and deed. But it is not in our *nature*. We are all afflicted with the disease of sin, but it is *in* us and not *of* us. When Paul writes about wrestling with sin in Romans 7, he makes it clear that it isn't his very nature that is sinful: "For I do not understand my own actions. For I do not do what I want, but I do the very thing I hate. Now if I do what I do not want, I agree with the law, that it is good. So now it is *no longer I* who do it, but sin *that dwells* within me" (Romans 7.15-17). Do you see what Paul says? It's not him - not his being, not his self, not his nature, but it is sin *in* him - sin is something "other." A few sentences later he writes, "For I delight in the law of God, in my inner being, but I see in my members another law waging war against the law of my mind and making me captive to the law of sin *that dwells* in my members" (22-23).

The word nature is important. Nature (whether you're translating the word *physis* or *ousius*) is *what we are* - it's the constitution of our being. We are human *beings*. If we were speaking physically, then we would be talking about our DNA - what constitutes us as humans and therefore distinguishes us from squids or apes or dandelions. I would argue that we do *not* have a sinful nature, but that we have a nature infected with sin. We are not, constitutionally, in our very being, sinful, but we have sin "in us."

The Augustinian doctrine of Original Sin leads to the West seeing humanity as being, *en masse*, unacceptable to a pure, holy, and righteous God, and thus due recipients of his just wrath. The East, on the other hand, sees God as wrathful, not toward our nature - not toward *us*, but toward the disease which afflicts us, and from which we must be healed. And this, of course, ends up with the Reformers seeing the cross as a transactional event in which God *punishes* Christ for *our* sins (because, with God at least - even though he teaches us the opposite, forgiveness requires payment). It ends up with the East seeing the cross as the epitome of God *taking away our sin* - Jesus, dying on the cross, causes sin to die with him, descending to hell he wreaks havoc on death itself (the consequence of sin), and rising again he conquers sin and death, and promises to do the same in humankind.

The Western view tends to put God the Father and God the Son at odds. You've heard of "good cop, bad cop"? This is "good God, bad God." God the Father, full of implacable justice, God the Son, offering himself as *payment* to appease him. Like I said before, it creates a kind of schizophrenic Deity. The Eastern view tends to put God the Father and God the Son "on the same page" - loving the world and doing everything in heaven's power to remedy the situation.

Ken

❊❊❊❊❊❊❊❊❊❊❊❊❊❊❊❊❊❊

Dear Ken:

You've given me a lot to chew on - I've never thought about sin as being "something other" that "infects" us. But, I'm not sure I completely agree with what you are saying. I mean, to put it in short words, we will sin, won't we? Isn't it in our nature to sin? I mean, maybe it isn't in our spiritual DNA, maybe it isn't in our very being, but isn't it our nature to sin? Isn't that just the way we are now?

Andy

❊❊❊❊❊❊❊❊❊❊❊❊❊❊❊❊❊❊

Dear Andy:

Yes, without question we will sin, because, as you say, that is "just the way we are now." But once more let me try to clarify what I'm saying. I would suggest that we are "the way we are now" because *all of us* (we got it from Grandpa Adam) have been "infected" with sin (not "sins," but "sin" - singular - sinfulness). But I would also suggest that the sinfulness we have inherited *isn't part of our nature* - it isn't part of our *being*.

Think about it. If sin is *really* part of our nature, then Jesus didn't become a *real* man. Hebrews 4.15 tells us, "For we do not have a high priest who is unable to sympathize with our weaknesses, but one who in every respect has been tempted as we are, *yet without sin*." If Jesus was "without sin," and yet sin is part of our *very nature*, then Jesus didn't become a real human being. If that's the case, he didn't live as one of us, die as one of us, or rise again as one of us. Hebrews also says, "Since therefore the children share in flesh and blood, he himself likewise partook of the same things, that through death he might destroy the one who has the power of death, that is, the devil, and deliver all those who through fear of death were subject to lifelong slavery" (2.14,15).

If sin is part of our very nature, then we can't say that God loves us, because God doesn't love sin. But if sin is a kind of spiritual malady, a spiritual disease or infection, then God can love us and detest our affliction, and do something about it! In short, sinfulness is not an essential part of what it means to be human.

God be with you,

Ken

❊❊❊❊❊❊❊❊❊❊❊❊❊❊❊❊❊

My dear Bishop Ken:

Let me say I am very much enjoying this discussion of ours, and I am growing from it. Thank you for your help, and I hope I'm not being too much of an inconvenience for you. I see now that it really doesn't make a lot of sense that sin is in our very nature. Yes, we have a predisposition to sin, and yes we are all sinners, but it isn't in our being. *I like what you said about us being "infected" with sin, and I would like for you to say more about that. But first, one of the questions you asked me to ponder earlier was in regard to how PSA seems to make God schizophrenic, and almost pits the Father against the Son. That idea has been troubling me ever since you asked it, and now I'm starting to have trouble reconciling a loving Father with the idea of a God who demands payment before forgiveness. Can you possibly elaborate on that theme a bit more?*

Andy

Chapter Four

Cur Deus Homo
Why God Became Man: The Rescue Plan

My dear Mr. Boso:

I trust all is well with you since we last corresponded. You asked me to elaborate on the theme of the Father's love for us, and I will be most happy to do so, for it is the most wonderful theme in all creation!

Shall we begin at the beginning? At the very heart of God? As I pointed out before, the most beloved verse in the entire Bible is John 3.16: "For God so loved the world, that he gave his only Son, that whoever believes in him should not perish but have eternal life."

The Heart Of The Father

I would like to point out that God becoming man was not some voluntary operation of the Son in contradistinction to the justice-demanding heart of the Father. The Son became man *because of* the heart of the Father. This is the reason the Son does anything and everything. Jesus said, "Truly, truly, I say to you, the Son can do nothing of his own accord, but only what he sees the Father doing. For whatever theFather does, that the Son does likewise" (John 5.19). Later he said, "When you have lifted up the Son of Man, then you will know that I am he, and that I do nothing on my own authority, but speak just as the Father taught me" (John 8.28). Everything the Son does is simply a publication, a showing forth, a revelation, of the heart of the Father. The reason the Son took on human nature is because the Father "so loved" the world.

This is not, by the way, a New Testament revelation. It's not as if God, in the Old Testament, was some kind of grumpy Deity, full of wrath and vengeance, who suddenly, come the New Testament, has a change of heart and becomes a nice guy. The inclination of God's heart *from the beginning* has not been about being paid in order to forgive us (if you would like, I'll talk more later about how we have misunderstood the whole idea of sacrifice in the Old Testament). When he revealed himself to Moses, he showed his heart's inclination: "The Lord passed before him and proclaimed, 'The Lord, the Lord, a God merciful and gracious, slow to anger, and abounding in steadfast love and faithfulness, keeping steadfast love for thousands, forgiving iniquity and transgression and sin, but who will by no means clear the guilty, visiting the iniquity of the fathers on the children and the children's children, to the third and the fourth generation'" (Exodus 34.6,7). Some people jump right to the end of that passage without letting the first part sink in. So, let's look for just a moment at the passage, and deal with the hard end part first.

"Who will by no means clear the guilty, visiting the iniquity of the fathers on the children and the children's children, to the third and the fourth generation." There are two things God says about himself which at first glance seem harsh and unforgiving. First, that he will by no means clear the guilty. But, didn't he just say he was forgiving? Of course he is. The point being made here, though, is that sins have consequences. If you think of salvation as simply canceling a debt because someone else (Jesus) paid it, or displacing a punishment because someone else (Jesus) took it, then this text makes no sense at all. If, on the other hand, you approach the text understanding that sins (plural; sinful thoughts, words and deeds) are the result of the disease of sin within us, then even if we are forgiven, there are still consequences. This is not simply an Old Testament idea that somehow gets replaced by grace in the New Testament. Paul himself - the Apostle of Grace - tells us that how we live our lives has repercussions: "Do not be deceived: God is not mocked, for *whatever one sows, that will he also reap*. For the one who sows to his own flesh will from the flesh reap corruption, but the one who sows to the Spirit will from the Spirit reap eternal life" (Galatians 6.7,8).

Paul also writes that we will *all* be tested as though by fire: "According to the grace of God given to me, like a skilled master builder I laid a foundation, and someone else is building upon it. Let each one take care how he builds upon it. For no one can lay a foundation other than that which is laid, which is Jesus Christ. Now if anyone builds on the foundation with gold, silver, precious stones, wood, hay, straw - each one's work will become manifest, for the Day will disclose it, because it will be revealed by fire, and *the fire will test what sort of work each one has done.* If the work that anyone has built on the foundation survives, he will receive a reward. If anyone's work is burned up, he will suffer loss, though he himself will be saved, but only as through fire" (1 Corinthians 3.10-15).

Mind you, Paul is writing all these things to Christians! He wrote it to people who were in Christ and who were forgiven of their sins. Finally, this verse: "For we must all appear before the judgment seat of Christ, so that each one may *receive what is due for what he has done in the body, whether good or evil*" (1 Corinthians 5.10).

My point is, even in the New Testament, there are consequences to our foolish, ungodly choices - there are consequences to our embracing the disease of sin rather than fighting it tooth and toenail. Both in this life, and according to Paul, in the life to come, there is a purging, a burning, a cleansing that must take place. But it is a burning of purification, not a burning of destruction.

Jesus, too, said the same thing: "For *everyone* will be salted with fire" (Mark 9.49).

But I digress. We were talking about what God said to Moses. He forgives us, but will by no means clear the guilty. We all reap what we sow.

God goes on to say something that has been completely misunderstood and misapplied, and has become a foundation for thinking that God punishes children for the sins of their fathers (*contra* what the Bible says elsewhere; see Deuteronomy 24.16 and Ezekiel 18.20). What the text actually says is that God will "visit the iniquities of the fathers...on the third and fourth generation." This is not a passage of threatening, it is a passage describing longsuffering. God will put up with sin, he will be patient, but eventually he will "visit" and deal with it. One generation walks contrary to God and teaches the next generation to do the same. Eventually ("the third and fourth generation") the sin becomes (to borrow James' words) "full grown" and the consequences come tumbling down on a family or a nation or a culture. But repentance can turn the tide - when people *stop* walking in wickedness things change for the better. There are still consequences (for example, broken families, disease, misery), but the fullness of consequences is alleviated.

OK, I said all that in order to be able to focus on what people usually just skip right over - the first part of the passage where God reveals himself to Moses: "The Lord, the Lord, a God merciful and gracious, slow to anger, and abounding in steadfast love and faithfulness, keeping steadfast love for thousands, forgiving iniquity and transgression and sin." God's heart of mercy and forgiveness and steadfast love isn't something kept secret until John 3.16. It is who God has declared and shown himself to be from the beginning. The Old Testament is riddled with this declaration, from the Pentateuch through the Prophets, and in all the Wisdom literature.

My point: the heart of the Father is lovingkindness. His heart's desire is *not* to demand payment or penalty, but to *heal* the sinfulness of humanity.

Well, that's probably enough to chew on for the moment. We can pick up the discussion after you've had some time for reflection.

God bless you, my friend,

Bishop Ken

❊❊❊❊❊❊❊❊❊❊❊❊❊❊❊❊❊❊

Dear Kenneth:

Thank you for that last post. I see now that God's heart is a heart of love and forgiveness. I even see how the consequences of our sins can bring about the fire of purification and cleansing and actually work in us God's purposes, burning away the disease and making us more like Jesus.

But this all leaves me a little confused as to why Jesus became man at all! I mean, if it wasn't to pay our debt or pay our penalty, then why did the Son need to become incarnate and die for us? Please help me understand this! I feel like I'm starting to get the picture, and at the same time, I feel like it's all starting to unravel in my mind. Help!

Very sincerely,

Andy

❊❊❊❊❊❊❊❊❊❊❊❊❊❊❊❊❊❊

Dear Andy:

I know how you feel! Someone once told me that, before you knock down the old pillars that hold up a structure, it's best to build the new pillars, otherwise the whole thing comes crashing down. You may feel like the pillars that have supported you are getting knocked down, and I had best hurry and give you some new pillars to hold your faith in place! Let me try to do that by lining out the two views (PSA, and the more biblical and ancient view) one after the other.

The Pillars of Satisfaction and PSA

Anselm, and the Reformers after him, saw what Christ did as a "satisfaction" to the dishonor God had received from man's sin, or as a penalty Christ paid God in order for God to forgive us. Jesus took the *punishment* for our sins on himself.

Pillar # 1: God Took Our Punishment On Himself

Maybe you've heard PSA described as a courtroom scene. It goes something like this: a judge saying, "You are guilty. *You* must pay."

And the guilty person saying, "But I *can't* pay!" So the judge says, "I know you can't. And I love you. So I will pay." The judge reaches into his wallet, pulls out $200, and pays the fine he has just levied and releases the guilty party. On closer inspection this story falls apart. Here's why: in this illustration the judge isn't the transcendent one. He is not paying *himself* - he is paying *someone else* - the state, the city, the court system, *someone* besides him is getting the payment. The judge takes the $200 out of his billfold, but he doesn't just put it in his other pocket, he gives it to someone or something *above and beyond* himself. But God isn't a judge who has someone over him - someone, some "thing," some "principle," even some "attribute," higher than himself. God is the Transcendent Lord of All. So, instead of using this illustration, let's change it up a bit...

The King of the Land - who owns everything in the realm, who answers to no one, and who's word is the law - says, "You are guilty so you must pay. You have broken my law, you have offended against my honor. You have stolen from me. You must pay." The guilty party says, "But I cannot pay! I have no money!" So the king says, "Yes, I know you cannot pay. But I love you. I will pay the penalty for you." And he gets out his billfold, pulls out $200, and gives it to...(ah, here's where it gets squirrelly)...himself. In other words - *there was no actual payment made, the king simply forgave the debt.*

If that illustration doesn't work for you, we can try this one. Same scenario, king and guilty. The penalty, however, is not monetary - it is ten years in prison, or if you like the story better with a stiffer penalty, it can be death.

The sentence is handed down. The king says, "The penalty must be paid, but I love you. So *I* will pay the penalty for you." So the king steps down from his throne and takes off his royal robes, and goes to prison for ten years (or, if you prefer, gets his head chopped off). Makes no sense at all - justice isn't served in this scenario, and the king doesn't just cut off his nose to spite his face, he cuts off his own head instead of just commuting the sentence.

AND THAT'S THE POINT! Retell the whole story once more. The sentencing comes: "Off with his head." And then the king, who's word is law, commutes the sentence. *No payment had to be made.*

To say that some payment *had to be made* in order for us to obtain forgiveness implies there is something (at least some standard) higher than the omnipotent God himself, and it also turns out that forgiveness isn't really forgiveness at all - payment of *some kind* was made (but more about that later).

Pillar # 2: Justice Was Served

"But justice must be served!" God is a God of justice, and justice has to be done in order to gain our forgiveness - so say the PSA folk. But is justice served by Christ dying to pay for our sins?

If you steal from me - say you break into my house and steal a treasured family heirloom, worth $200,000 (but which I would never ever sell because it was worth even more to me - it was invaluable), you get caught, and go on trial. But between the time you stole my treasure and got caught, you pawned it somewhere for $6,000, then went and blew that money on a nice week in Paris. Now, you go before the judge (or the king), and you get sentenced to life in prison. What good is that to me? Has justice been served *from my perspective*? Has anything been "made right"? No. Punishment has been meted out, but justice hasn't occurred. The biblical notion of justice is not "a penalty being meted out," but, "things being made right." If Christ *paid a penalty* on our behalf, and things still haven't been "made right," then justice hasn't really been served. But, if what Christ did was *take our sin* into his death, and reconcile us to the Father, then the process of "making all things new," or making all things *right*, has begun.

Pillar # 3: Christ Died, Then God Forgave

Back to this, then. No, he didn't forgive. Satisfaction was demanded. "I'll forgive you, but first someone has to pay," are the words we put in God's mouth. We would teach our children, if they said this, that this wasn't real forgiveness - "Daddy, Johnny broke my light saber, I'll forgive him, but first he has to buy me a new one." But then we turn right around and say this is precisely how God acts. Why would we say that? Because the theological construct we have embraced says that about him.

True forgiveness is dismissing the offense. "Forgive us our trespasses (or as some say, "debts"), as we forgive those who trespass against us." For heaven's sake, we pray this prayer that Jesus taught us! God's kind of forgiveness and our kind of forgiveness should be the *same* kind of forgiveness. But instead we are told that *we* should forgive without seeking payment, but God forgives only after payment has been made - granted, payment that we ourselves were incapable of making, so the Son makes it for us, and the payment is death itself. However, the Bible tells us that because we have been forgiven by God, we, *in the same way*, should forgive others. Jesus made this point in The Parable Of The Unforgiving Servant (I know you may be tempted to skip the text, but please take time to read it):

> Then Peter came up and said to him, "Lord, how often will my brother sin against me, and I forgive him? As many as seven times?" Jesus said to him, "I do not say to you seven times, but seventy-seven times.
>
> "Therefore the kingdom of heaven may be compared to a king who wished to settle accounts with his servants. When he began to settle, one was brought to him who owed him ten thousand talents. And since he could not pay, his master ordered him to be sold, with his wife and children and all that he had, and payment to be made. So the servant fell on his knees, imploring him, 'Have patience with me, and I will pay you everything.' And out

of pity for him, the master of that servant released him and *forgave him the debt*. But when that same servant went out, he found one of his fellow servants who owed him a hundred denarii, and seizing him, he began to choke him, saying, 'Pay what you owe.' So his fellow servant fell down and pleaded with him, 'Have patience with me, and I will pay you.' He refused and went and put him in prison until he should pay the debt. When his fellow servants saw what had taken place, they were greatly distressed, and they went and reported to their master all that had taken place. Then his master summoned him and said to him, 'You wicked servant! I forgave you all that debt because you pleaded with me. And should not you have had mercy on your fellow servant, as I had mercy on you?' And in anger his master delivered him to the jailers, until he should pay all his debt. So also my heavenly Father will do to every one of you, if you do not forgive your brother from your heart" (Matthew 18.21-35).

Forgiveness does not necessitate payment. In fact, it particularly dismisses payment.

And that is the point - we can say either "payment was made" or "forgiveness was given." But we can't say both. The two are mutually exclusive.

If, on the other hand, we see what Christ accomplished not as paying a penalty which the Father demanded (thus putting a kind of conflict between the Father and the Son) and which we couldn't pay - if we do away with the notion of penalty completely - and instead see this as a rescue operation from the heart of the Father, through the action of the Son, to come into our world, to become one of us, not to avert God's wrath toward us, but to *rescue us from our sin*, then it all makes sense. We've been telling the wrong story when we talk about the judge or the king and the trial and penalty. The right story is that we were spiritually sick unto death, and God despised, not us, but the sickness which was laying us waste. And he took on our humanity, suffered the consequences of the sickness itself ("For our sake he made him to be sin who knew no sin, so that in him we might become the righteousness of God," Paul tells us in 2 Corinthians 5.21) and died - but he conquered death, rose victorious, defeating sin, hell, and death. And then he inoculates us with a transfusion of his resurrection life, and begins working in us a healing that gradually conquers the power and effect of sin, and on the last day will conquer in us death itself.

It is a rescue operation, from beginning to end.

Well, my friend, I'm guessing that is enough for the moment. I have attempted to dismantle the pillars of PSA - in the next letter I hope to quickly put up some new pillars to support your faith.

Ken

❈ ❈ ❈ ❈ ❈ ❈ ❈ ❈ ❈ ❈ ❈ ❈ ❈ ❈ ❈ ❈ ❈ ❈

Dear Ken:

OK. I'm ready for the new pillars, but don't waste much time! I feel the roof around me starting to fall and I need some support. I see now that the pillars of PSA have been pretty weak. I was talking to an atheist friend of mine about our faith, and I let him read what you wrote. Maybe you will appreciate what he said: "Wow! That blew my mind! He just cleared up one of the big issues I have with Christianity. Tell him thank you."

So, my friend, I'm placing my order for new pillars. Please don't delay in delivery.

Your friend,
Andy

❋ ❋ ❋ ❋ ❋ ❋ ❋ ❋ ❋ ❋ ❋ ❋ ❋ ❋ ❋ ❋ ❋ ❋

Dear Andy:

The comment from your atheist friend made my day! I pray that he will come believe that God *is*, and to see and embrace the love God has for him. You've asked for new pillars, and now I hope to deliver them *post haste*.

In Matthew 1.20-21 we read "But as [Joseph] considered these things, behold, an angel of the Lord appeared to him in a dream, saying, 'Joseph, son of David, do not fear to take Mary as your wife, for that which is conceived in her is from the Holy Spirit. She will bear a son, and you shall call his name Jesus, for he will save his people from their sins.'"

Notice the last phrase in particular: "He shall save his people from their sins."

This text sometimes gets read at Christmas. But if our Christmas thoughts go no deeper than sentimentalism - gentle Jesus lying in a manger, a sweet mother with a sweet child, a picture of warmth and maternity and innocence, then we have done a disservice to the event, for this was no typical mother and this was no typical child. Here was a virgin - bringing forth a son, and here was a son, not of some man, but of God himself, who would, the angel told Joseph, "save his people from their sins." The question before us is, *how* does this child of Mary save his people from their sins?

Pillar # 1: Humanity Was Infected With Sin

"It will kill you," not, "I will kill you." It is amazing the difference one little letter can make in a sentence - but the "t" in "It" is of major importance. When God placed Adam and Eve in the Garden of Eden he told them to freely eat from any tree in the Garden except one - the tree of the knowledge of good and evil. Of course, we all know the story - the first couple disobeyed God and ate from the one tree they shouldn't have. The consequence was death, not only for them, but for everyone who would come after them. Death was unleashed upon humanity. Paul writes, "...sin came into the world through one man, and death through sin, and so death spread to all men because all sinned" (Romans 5.12).

It is important to notice God gave them a *warning*, not a *threat*. He did not say, "If you eat from the tree, I will kill you." He said, "but of the tree of the knowledge of good and evil you shall not eat, for in the day that you eat of it you shall surely die" (Genesis 2.17). Here is the difference between a warning and a threat: you have a three year old child in your household and you say to her, "Whatever you do, don't put anything in that electrical outlet, or else you will die!" The child proceeds, as soon as you have turned your back, to stick a fork right into the outlet. Zap! She screams. You run to her. She's alive but terrified. If your statement to her was a warning, so be it. Fortunately she *didn't* die, and chances are she will never do that again. If, on the other hand, your statement to her was a threat, then you go to the kitchen, get a big knife, and plunge it into her heart - you *told* her she would die if she disobeyed you!

What kind of father *is* this, who would threaten a child rather than warn a child? We would call such a father abusive and twisted and mentally off his rocker, yet we attribute precisely the same characteristics to God and call him good.

Coincidentally, Dennis Henderson, a pastor friend of mine just came by and I wrote the "change one letter" sentence for him:

"It will kill you."

"I will kill you."

I asked him, "Why is it that we read the verse in Genesis as a threat instead of a warning? Maybe it has something to do with not only Anselm's theology, but also his psychology, seeing that his father was so oppressive and abusive that Anselm left home and took up a wild life as a teenager. And yet, this is very much the picture of God that we have painted." My friend Dennis replied, "Unlike the picture of God that Jesus himself painted in the Parable of the Prodigal Son." Exactly! Jesus portrays God as a loving, reconciling, forgiving Father. We have portrayed him as a monster.

Let me bring us back to the point: Adam disobeyed God and sin entered the world and through sin, death entered. Adam and Eve were infected with a spiritual malady. They passed it on to their children. Everyone sins (because we have the spiritual disease of sin) and everyone dies. What we need is not a course on ethics, we need healing. We need saving! But since every last one of us has the disease, there is no way for us to conquer it. We need healing from beyond.

Pillar # 2: God Became Man

Adam sinned, humanity fell into sin and death, and we needed a healer, a rescuer, a savior from beyond to come to our help.

Andy, this may be the most important sentence I write you in the entire course of our conversation: *Our focus must shift from the anger of God to the desperation of humanity.* God sent his Son into this world, *not* to "pay our debt" or "suffer our penalty" - both of which are focused on appeasing an angry or offended Father. God sent his Son into this word, because he *loved* us and intended to do something to change our condition! Once again, the famous verse, this time with the next verse added in for good measure: "For God so loved the world, that he gave his only Son, that whoever believes in him should not perish but have eternal life. For God did not send his Son into the world to condemn the world, but in order that the world might be saved through him" (John 3.16,17).

Just as a little theological experiment, reduce those verses, dropping the middle section: "For God so loved the world, that he gave his only Son...in order that the world might be saved through him."

Again, the heart of the Father is not an offended heart that must be appeased, but a loving heart that *actively* loves.

So God becomes man in Jesus Christ. He is Immanuel, "God with us." He took on our nature - fully (again, if sin is part of our nature instead of a dreaded spiritual infirmity, then the Son didn't assume our full nature). He was "born of a woman, born under the Law" (Galatians 4.4).

The sacrifice of Christ didn't begin on the cross, it began in the Incarnation. Much Western theology (and this may be from the Church of Rome or the Baptist church down the street, or anywhere in between) focuses so particularly on the event of Jesus' death (and a glorious event it was!) that they fail to see that the very act of God becoming man was a sacrifice in itself. The heart of the Father is a giving heart, not an offended heart.

Pillar # 3: Jesus Took Away Our Sin

The Son sacrificed himself...

Wait a minute! It just dawned on me that we can't even talk about sacrifice without making it into some kind of "payment" or "penalty." We have been so steeped in PSA that the very notion of Christ sacrificing himself is, in our minds, Christ sacrificing himself *to* someone - and in this case, *to the Father*. But think of sacrifice in different terms. Instead of *to* someone, think of it as *for* someone.

Remember that three year old child you warned not to stick the fork into the outlet? She does it anyway but fortunately survives. Six weeks later, you are walking down the sidewalk and she steps into the street in front of an oncoming bus. Without hesitation, because you love her with all your heart, you lunge in front of the bus, push her to safety, and are yourself hit by the Greyhound and left with a broken leg, three cracked ribs and a headache that lasts for weeks. You sacrificed yourself - not *to* someone, but *for* someone. It happens all the time in lesser and greater degrees. A wife sacrifices an evening and her delicate sense of good music, so she can take her husband to go see Bob Dylan in concert; a dad sacrifices buying a new car so he can provide a money for college tuition for his daughter; a soldier sacrifices his life so his countrymen can enjoy freedom. None of these sacrifices are made in order to appease someone, they are made from a heart of love - "Greater love has no one than this, that someone lay down his life for a friend" (John 15.13).

Where did I leave off? Oh - the Son sacrificed himself as an act of rescue. He sacrificed himself by taking on our human nature, and by taking on our human ailment. "For our sake he made him to be sin who knew no sin, so that in him we might become the righteousness of God" (2 Corinthians 5.21). Jesus took on our condition (though he did not sin), and the results of it were the same as ours: he died. Dead. Really and truly dead. Not kind of dead. Not partly dead. Dead dead. Descend to the place of death dead. The disease had the same effect on him as it has on us. It killed him.

But on the third day Jesus rose from the dead. What? A dead man defeated death!

How can this be? Jesus conquered death! No one else had ever beat the disease, no one else had ever defeated sin and death. But this man, Jesus the Christ, did just that. He rose from the dead announcing himself as the *antidote* to our deadly disease!

In that one, whole, fluid, movement from heaven to earth, to hell, to earth, and back to heaven - from incarnation to death, to descent into hell, to resurrection, to ascension - Jesus fulfilled the words of John the Baptist: "Behold, the lamb of God, who takes away the sin of the world" (John 1.29).

By knowing him experientially, through conversion, through the Word of God, through the process of sanctification, through the Sacraments, we are constantly receiving the antidote to our disease. He washes us in healing waters, he gives us a spiritual blood transfusion - think about Holy Communion in *this* light! Paul wrote (in 1 Corinthians 10.16), "The cup of blessing that we bless, is it not a participation in the blood of Christ? The bread that we break, is it not a participation in the body of Christ?" Peter writes, "you may become partakers of the divine nature, having escaped from the corruption that is in the world because of sinful desire" (2 Peter 1.4b).

Christ conquered death, then gives us an injection of *his* spiritual DNA!

We are not all the way healed yet. But we are getting better. Sin is losing its power over us. And on the Last Day we will join Jesus in his victory over death. We will kick the grave in the teeth, we will overcome as he overcame. We will put on immortality. Because - a baby - was born - among us.

Andy, you grew up in Switzerland - have you traveled through Europe much? Have you been to El Mezquita in Cordoba, Spain? When it was built it was the largest mosque in the world, and now it is a Christian church. It is one of the most amazing buildings I have ever been in. When you walk in you are immediately overwhelmed by the number of columns in the place - it seems like there must be a thousand. I've only given you a few pillars here for a different way of looking at what Christ accomplished, and perhaps these will suffice to at least hold up the structure of your faith. But I must tell you that the more you read the Scriptures in this light, the more columns you will find to strengthen your understanding. It seems to me that nearly every time I pick up my Bible I see something else that confirms this message of the loving heart of the Father and the rescue mission of the Son.

Obviously there are some passages in the Bible that give a person pause. This happens no matter what subject we are looking at. But the more I study the Word of God in this light, even the texts that at first seemed contrary to what I'm saying suddenly fall in place as supportive columns. I hope it will be the same for you.

Please don't hesitate to write back if you have more thoughts.

God bless you,

Kenneth

Chapter Five

Propitiation And Sacrifice
They Don't Mean
What You Think They Mean

Dear Bishop:

I very much appreciate that last letter. It answered a lot of questions, and it did give me some pillars to replace the old ones with. By the way, yes, I have been to El Mezquita. One thing that impressed me was the vivid life and color on the columns and walls in the "church" part - all covered with paintings of saints and angels, in contrast to the staid orange and white designs on the rest of the columns. It really shows the life *found in the Christian faith!*

You said in your last letter that the more you read the Scriptures the more this view of the Atonement made sense to you. I think I'm having exactly the opposite experience. For sure, some of the texts I read really make more sense when I read them in this light, but there are a few very significant passages that seem to take a chainsaw to your pillars. It's almost like they stand there in the Bible as bold proof that what you are saying is wrong, or at least very incomplete. In fact, after reading and re-reading our ongoing discussion, and giving a lot of thought to what you have said, I am almost coming to the conclusion that the Bible itself waffles on what Christ accomplished. I just can't get away from the penalty *idea - that Christ took the* punishment *due to us. But I also can't embrace that idea anymore. I don't know if you can help me with these passages, because they seem pretty clear to me, but I'm willing to let you give it a shot.*

First, there are those memorable verses from The Song of the Suffering Savior, *in Isaiah 53 which, as I understand it, prophesy the suffering of the Messiah on our behalf. It is a long passage that, from what I can understand, very clearly states that the Messiah was* punished *for us:*

> *4 Surely he has borne our griefs*
>   *and carried our sorrows;*
> *yet we esteemed him stricken,*
>   *smitten by God, and afflicted.*
> *5 But he was pierced for our transgressions;*
>   *he was crushed for our iniquities;*
> *upon him was the chastisement that brought us peace,*
>   *and with his wounds we are healed.*
> *6 All we like sheep have gone astray;*
>   *we have turned—every one—to his own way;*
> *and the Lord has laid on him*
>   *the iniquity of us all.*
> *7 He was oppressed, and he was afflicted,*
>   *yet he opened not his mouth;*
> *like a lamb that is led to the slaughter,*
>   *and like a sheep that before its shearers is silent,*
>   *so he opened not his mouth.*
> *8 By oppression and judgment he was taken away;*
>   *and as for his generation, who considered*

that he was cut off out of the land of the living,
    stricken for the transgression of my people?
9 And they made his grave with the wicked
    and with a rich man in his death,
although he had done no violence,
    and there was no deceit in his mouth.
10 Yet it was the will of the Lord to crush him;
    he has put him to grief;
when his soul makes an offering for guilt,
    he shall see his offspring; he shall prolong his days;
the will of the Lord shall prosper in his hand.
11 Out of the anguish of his soul he shall see and be satisfied;
by his knowledge shall the righteous one, my servant,
    make many to be accounted righteous,
    and he shall bear their iniquities.
12 Therefore I will divide him a portion with the many,
    and he shall divide the spoil with the strong,
because he poured out his soul to death
    and was numbered with the

transgressors;
yet he bore the sin of many,
   and makes intercession for the transgressors.

The parts that trouble me:

•We esteemed him smitten, stricken by God...

•Upon him was the chastisement that brought us peace...

•The Lord has laid on him the iniquity of us all...

•Stricken for the transgression of my people...

•It was the will of the Lord to crush him...

•When his soul makes an offering for guilt...

•He shall bear their iniquities...

This also brings up, for me, the whole question of Jewish sacrifices. Weren't these "forerunners" or "examples" or "types" for the sacrifice of Christ which was to come? Didn't God command that sacrifices be offered to him? And weren't these sacrifices made in order to obtain forgiveness from God? How does this square with what you are saying?

The other Scriptures that almost prove the PSA understanding are from the New Testament, and all have the word "propitiation" in them:

> *Romans 3.25: ...whom God put forward as a propitiation by his blood, to be received by faith. This was to show God's righteousness, because in his divine forbearance he had passed over former sins.*

> *Hebrews 2.17: Therefore he had to be made like his brothers in every respect, so that he might become a merciful and faithful high priest in the service of God, to make propitiation for the sins of the people.*

> *1 John 2.2: He is the propitiation for our sins, and not for ours only but also for the sins of the whole world.*

1 John 4.10: In this is love, not that we have loved God but that he loved us and sent his Son to be the propitiation for our sins.

The dictionary definition of "propitiation" is, "The action of appeasing a god, spirit, or person." It just seems to fly in the face of what you are telling me.

Quite honestly, I am beginning to feel like El Mezquita myself - I have an overabundance of pillars, and some of them don't match the rest of them!

Help me if you can,

Andy

❊ ❊ ❊ ❊ ❊ ❊ ❊ ❊ ❊ ❊ ❊ ❊ ❊ ❊ ❊ ❊ ❊

Dear Andy:

Oh man, just reading your letter nearly wore me out, let alone thinking about how to reply to it. There are so many things to say in response that I don't know where to begin.

Allow me to think out loud for a minute. I think what I will do is attempt to answer your questions backwards. I will start with the New Testament "propitiation" verses, I will talk a little bit about the Jewish sacrificial system, then I will tackle that formidable passage from Isaiah. All along I'll be praying for God to give me clarity in my writing, because there is a danger of this being so involved that it becomes a complicated mess. My fear is that my words make things *more* confusing for you instead of bringing clarity. Nevertheless, I am about to jump off into the deep end!

Propitiation

All four of the passages you cited (from three different New Testament writers, no less) say unequivocally that Jesus is the propitiation for our sins. The question is, then, what does propitiation mean?

Please bear with me while as I attempt to unpack the word a little bit. Quite honestly, this word was a *huge* monkey wrench in my thinking when I was transitioning from just being uncomfortable and unsatisfied with PSA to arriving at a place of saying, "No, I simply don't believe it anymore."

You are correct about the dictionary definition. Here is what I found:

Propitiation: Noun - The action of propitiating or appeasing a god, spirit, or person.

Propitiate: Verb - To win or regain the favor of (a god, spirit, or person) by doing something that pleases them. Synonyms: placate - appease - conciliate - pacify - mollify.

So, if we accept at face value the English definition, Jesus died on the cross to "placate, appease, conciliate, pacify, mollify" the Father. But I suggest we leave behind English for a moment and dig in to the word these writers actually used.

In Greek the word is *hilasterion*. In the pagan Greek culture the word is indeed used for appeasing an angry God. But in the *Septuagint* (the Old Testament translation used by the Apostles - the one they quoted when they gave Old Testament references in their writings) *hilasterion* is the word for "mercy seat." in Exodus. Remember, the Ark of the Covenant contained a copy of the Law (*the* copy of the Law), and the mercy seat was the "lid" to the Ark. The Law demands our perfection, but the mercy seat covered those demands - and it was there that blood was sprinkled on the Day of Atonement.

Now, the question is, when the New Testament writers (John, Paul, and whoever wrote Hebrews) use *hilasterion* are they referring to it from a pagan Greek definition (appeasing an angry God) or from an Old Testament *Septuagint* definition (covering to protect us in our failure to measure up to the Law)? Remember, these three writers were all Jews. My money is on the latter choice. Go back now and re-read those verses in light of what I've just shared.

So, Christ is the *hilasterion* - the "covering" - that protects us from the curse of the Law. He is the place where the blood of atonement is sprinkled, spilled, shed. Once again, the focus shifts - the idea is not that Christ died to change the Father (isn't he unchanging?), but to change us. His sacrifice of himself, initiated in the very heart of the Father, is our covering and our atonement.

You know what? I am just now reminded of a letter I wrote someone about this very subject, and I am going to share the entire letter with you. It will be a little repetitive, but repetition is good for learning, yes? Also, I tried to be cute and make a reference to a Dylan song, so if you don't "get" it, just ignore it. The letter starts off talking about God telling Abraham to sacrifice Isaac. Here it is:

> OK, before we get to the word and its definition, a little theological/philosophical background. God is not like the pagan gods who have to be "bought off" or else they will wreak havoc on life, limb and property. Think of Abraham offering Isaac - God tells him "take your son and offer him as a sacrifice." That's unthinkable to us. Doesn't jive with our sense of justice or anything else. Seems barbaric. *Is* barbaric. And that's the point. God says, "Offer your son," to Abraham, who is from a pagan culture - that's *the norm* in pagan culture, so Abe says, "Where do you want this killing done?" And God says, "Out on Highway 61." - Oh, wait, I digress. Where was I?
>
> Oh yes, so Abraham is going to follow through with the *pagan* tradition, and he gets on top of the mountain and God *stops him.* "Abe, this ain't the way we do things. This is *not* how you relate

to me. You don't buy me off by killing your boy. I'm not your father's kind of God." *Paradigm shift* - a God who isn't pleased with the blood of bulls and goats (or children), but who instead sacrifices *himself* for our wholeness.

So, if we approach the word *propitiation* (Greek: *hilasterion*) as some kind of religious bribe to appease an angry God, we are making God out to be like the pagan gods who need mollifying. This is not how he describes himself in the least - "longsuffering" and "full of mercy" and "forgiving thousands" and all those other words he uses to describe himself. He is *just* - yes, and *righteous* yes - but a *just* and *righteous* judge *makes things right* - he doesn't need buying off. God isn't the kind of God who demands payment. He specifically teaches us *against* such attitudes (you know - all the "forgive seventy times seven," "love your enemies," and "don't pay back evil with evil" lessons). He is the kind of God who, instead of demanding payment be made, actually sacrifices himself in order to reconcile sinners to himself.

Propitiation (*hilasterion*) ought not be interpreted with a *pagan* understanding, but with a biblical one. The word is used, in the *Septuagint* (and in Hebrews) for "the mercy seat." The seat (*of mercy*, mind you) that "covers" the ark which held the Law. The raw power of the Law would condemn us (all have sinned), but Christ is our "mercy seat" - he is the covering. Christ's sacrifice of himself is *not* a sacrifice *to* the Father, but a sacrifice to rescue us from sin. It is not "payment" to an angry deity. It is sacrifice of self in order to save. If you had a child you loved (a son or daughter or niece or nephew) who stepped in front of an oncoming semi-truck, you would sacrifice yourself to save the child, but you wouldn't be offering *payment* to anyone in order to save the child. So it is with the sacrifice of Christ. He is the *propitiation* (*hilasterion*) - the mercy seat, the covering - ***for our sins***, and not the pagan styling of propitiation - paying an angry god.

Jewish Sacrifices

Andy, you obviously have a good head on your shoulders, and you have thought through much of this in a deep way, where others might simply accept what I am saying at face value. I applaud you for your tenacity and your thoughtfulness. You are correct that the Jewish religious system revolved around sacrifices, and that these were commanded by God for the people of Israel. There are far too many sacrifices for us to get into here, and most of them had nothing to do with sin, and nothing to do with blood. But that is a discussion for another time. Suffice it to say that sacrifices were *central* in Jewish worship.

And yet, we also read in the Old Testament that what God is really after is not sacrifices and burnt offerings, but *relationship:*

> Psalm 40.6-8: "In sacrifice and offering you have not delighted, but you have given me an open ear. Burnt offering and sin offering you have not required. Then I said, 'Behold, I have come; in the scroll of the book it is written of me: I delight to do your will, O my God; your law is within my heart.'"

Isaiah 1.11: "What to me is the multitude of your sacrifices? says the Lord; I have had enough of burnt offerings of rams and the fat of well-fed beasts; I do not delight in the blood of bulls, or of lambs, or of goats."

Jeremiah 7.21,22: "For in the day that I brought them out of the land of Egypt, I did not speak to your fathers or command them concerning burnt offerings and sacrifices. But this command I gave them: 'Obey my voice, and I will be your God, and you shall be my people. And walk in all the way that I command you, that it may be well with you.'"

Hosea 6.6: "For I desire steadfast love and not sacrifice, the knowledge of God rather than burnt offerings."

Now, jump to the New Testament. In the Gospel of Mark one of the scribes asks Jesus what is the greatest commandment. Jesus told him, "The most important is, 'Hear, O Israel: The Lord our God, the Lord is one. And you shall love the Lord your God with all your heart and with all your soul and with all your mind and with all your strength.' The second is this: 'You shall love your neighbor as yourself.' There is no other commandment greater than these." Notice, Andy, there is nothing in these two "great commandments" about sacrifices. They are about love and relationship and doing good.

So, the scribe says to Jesus, "You are right, Teacher. You have truly said that he is one, and there is no other besides him. And to love him with all the heart and with all the understanding and with all the strength, and to love one's neighbor as oneself, *is much more than all whole burnt offerings and sacrifices*." This guy "got it." He understood that what God was looking for was not the technical observation of religious ceremony with sacrifices, but living a life of goodness and loving God. Jesus was impressed with this scribe: "And when Jesus saw that he answered wisely, he said to him, "You are not far from the kingdom of God" (Mark 12.28-34).

Whatever else we say about sacrifices in the Old Testament, as important as they were, *sacrifices were secondary*. What really counted was living a loving life toward God and toward others.

But there is more. The Jews didn't see sacrifices as actually dealing with sin. The writer of Hebrews tells us, "For it is impossible for the blood of bulls and goats to take away sins" (10.4).

What I have been taught and believed is that the Jews see sacrifices as appeasing God. That fits nicely with the PSA understanding of things. But, it turns out, what I was taught and believed is wrong.

I decided to go get my information "straight from the horse's mouth." I wrote several Jewish scholars with a question. Here is what I wrote:

> I am a product of Western Christianity which has placed a strong emphasis on what is called *Penal Substitutionary Atonement* - the doctrine that Christ died (a) in our place, (b) as payment of a penalty, (c) to appease God's just wrath.
>
> Now, *early* Christianity doesn't have this doctrine. And later Christians who developed and held to this doctrine use the argument that ancient Jewish blood sacrifices are evidence that God's righteous anger must be appeased.

So, can anyone help me? What is the purpose of blood sacrifices in ancient Jewish theology?

Andy, I have to tell you, I was *shocked* by their answers. What they told me, all of them, in a nutshell, is that sacrificing in order to appease God's anger is a concept completely foreign to them, and they see it as a "Christian invention." I pointed out to them that it was a *late* Christian invention, because the early Christians didn't see things this way either.

What purpose, then do the sacrifices serve? One fellow responded, "Strictly speaking it makes no logical sense that God needs anything from us nor that by giving God something we can absolve sins. I understand sacrifices by what they cause *for the people*. As biblical Jews were largely agrarians, sacrifices that involved animals and fruits/vegetables were significant and doing so both inspired awe and demonstrated an amount of relinquishing."

When asked, "Were animal sacrifices made to appease God and avert God's wrath, or were they made to cleanse people from sin?" another Jewish fellow responded, "Neither. Both of your possibilities assume that God is lacking something and requires it of us. The sacrifice is *for the one offering it*. A visceral experience to graft a contact action(with a monetary cost) onto the abstract notion of repentance." Another wrote, "I'll chime in my concurrence with the above answers. To reduce it to a very simplistic level the sin offerings were a punitive measure against the sinner as well as a method to force them to think about what they had done. There is no mystical voodoo going on that the act of the animal sacrifice actually forgives the sin in any way."

Another Jewish friend made it clear for me. He said, "When the Jews in the Old Testament were commanded to offer a lamb, it had to be spotless. This means it couldn't be just any lamb from the flock. It had to be raised separately. It had to be inspected every day and cared for. You had to look it in the eyes. This lamb had a *name* - it was a pet. When you offered it as a sacrifice, it *hurt*. It cost you something. The purposes of sacrifices was not to appease God or buy forgiveness. The purpose of sacrifices was to make you feel the cost and pain of your sin. God is a forgiving God. He doesn't need sacrifices in order to forgive sins, he just needs to be asked. The sacrifices are for us, not for him."

So what? Why do I share all this Jewish thought? What do we *do* with this? Let me conclude this section by bringing the focus back to Christ. If we see his sacrifice as an appeasement, to placate God's wrath, then we are saying something *new* - something neither the Jews nor the early Christians said. If, on the other hand, we see Christ's sacrifice as the same kind of sacrifice a loving parent makes for a child, then the sacrifice isn't *Godward* - it is instead *a selfless act made to accomplish something*. And the "something," in this case, is the doing away with sin. The Son of God took on humanity, took on our infirmity, took on our "smittenness," took on our sin (the spiritual disease) and our sins (the ungodly and wrong thoughts, words and deeds resulting from our condition), took on our very death, and bore them all on the cross. He sacrificed himself for us. Or, as the writer of Hebrews says, "He put away sin by the sacrifice of himself" (9.23).

Isaiah 53

This has been a terribly long response to your letter (which wasn't so short itself!), so if you need to take a break and read the rest of this later, I'll understand. No need to hurry a reply. But as I promised I want to deal with the Isaiah 53 passage you mentioned. When we revisit the passage in light of everything I've written here, it begins to come into a clearer, non-PSA focus. I'll take your bullet points and try to answer them as briefly as I can.

• *We esteemed him smitten, stricken by God...*

This one is fairly easy. "We esteemed him...stricken by God." It doesn't say he *was* stricken by God, but that's how we esteemed him. But what does "stricken by God" mean? It means to bear the consequences of our sins, and Christ did bear the consequences of our sins, though he was not a sinner. It wasn't an act of appeasement, it was an act of rescue.

• *Upon him was the chastisement that brought us peace...*

Fairly easy too. It's saying the same thing as the first bullet point, only in different words. But it brings up an important point. There is a difference between retributive punishment and chastisement. A parent may chastise a child in order to teach him, in order to change him, in order to make him better. But this is certainly not punitive or retributive. In taking our sin (and sins) upon himself, Christ suffered the consequences of our sin.

The *New American Standard Bible* (the most accurate translation in the English language) translates this passage, "The chastening *for our well-being* fell upon Him."

• *The Lord has laid on him the iniquity of us all...*

Also easy! Our sinful condition (which we inherited from Adam) causes us to act with iniquity - to commit actual sins. Christ took our sin and our sins on himself. "For our sake he made him to be sin who knew no sin, so that in him we might become the righteousness of God" (2 Corinthians 5.21).

• *Stricken for the transgression of my people...*

Stricken, yes. But by whom? God? Or Roman soldiers?

• *It was the will of the Lord to crush him...*

Indeed it was. That is the whole point of everything I've been writing to you. It was the will of the Father that the Son take on our sin and the consequences of our sin (up to and including death) in order to provide our rescue, not in order to appease God.

• *When his soul makes an offering for guilt...*

Finally, we *are* guilty of sin, and his sacrifice of himself causes us to see the great cost of our wickedness. But again, sacrifices *are for us*, not for God. Christ offered himself for our guilt, and the sacrifice of his life brings us to love him more, serve him more, and say no to the things and ways of the world which are opposed to the things and ways of God. Saint Paul put it this way, "For the grace of God has appeared, bringing salvation for all people, training us to renounce ungodliness and worldly passions, and to live self-controlled, upright, and godly lives in the present age, waiting for our blessed hope, the appearing of the glory of our great God and Savior Jesus Christ, who gave himself for us to redeem us from all lawlessness and to purify for himself a people for his own possession who are zealous for good works" (Titus 2.11-14).

Well, my friend, I hope this letter is as helpful as it is long. I must admit I am exhausted from writing it. I hope you haven't become exhausted in reading it!

"And now the *grace* of the Lord Jesus Christ, the *love* of God, and the *fellowship* of the Holy Spirit be with you,"

Kenneth

Chapter Six

The Process Of Being Saved

Dear Kenneth:

You cannot imagine how much that last letter helped me. You are absolutely correct - it was exhausting reading! I couldn't just skim through it, I had to think carefully about every line in the letter, but it clarified so much for me, and showed me just how deep-rooted our biases are when it comes to reading Scripture. I suppose this is unavoidable, but I believe, in light of what you have written, that I will be able to approach other troublesome passages as they arise, "through new glasses," so to speak.

I have one final question for you, if you would be so kind as to give me one more response. This question really isn't about theories of the Atonement, but it is related, I think. I would like for you to share your thoughts about the process of salvation. As I have pondered what you have shared, something has begun stirring in the back of my mind. It seems to me that in my Christian experience salvation is seen as a once and for all thing. What I mean is this: with the PSA focus on Christ "paying our debt" or "suffering our punishment," the only thing we had to do to "be saved" was to accept that fact in our hearts. When we accept that we are sinners in need of a savior, when we accept that Christ has "paid" for our salvation, then we are saved. I know it works differently in different churches' understanding, but that is essentially the idea. I accept Christ as my personal Lord and Savior, and I am saved. I'm saved from hell and I'm bound for heaven.

But if what you are saying is true (and I now am convinced that it is), it seems to me that salvation has to be more than just accepting Christ - it seems to me that salvation is more of a process than a punctiliar event. What leads me to this conclusion was something you said a couple of times, about how Christ is the antidote to sin and death and that as we grow in relationship we grow in victory over sin. You said, "We are not all the way healed yet. But we are getting better. Sin is losing its power over us. And on the Last Day we will join Jesus in his victory over death."

Would you do me the final kindness of talking to me a little bit about salvation as a process?

Thank you for all your words,

Andy

❋❋❋❋❋❋❋❋❋❋❋❋❋❋❋❋❋

Dear Andy:

It would be my pleasure to say a little about the process of salvation, but I must tell you that it will be just that - a little.

Saved From What?

In much of modern day Christianity, salvation has become a matter of having a "get out of hell free" card. The goal of many preachers is to "get people saved," and by that they mean, get people to "make a decision for Christ" or "pray the sinner's prayer" or "get baptized" - in order to avoid going to hell when they die, and instead go to heaven.

The interesting thing is, this isn't found in *any* of the apostolic sermons. There are seven sermons preached in the book of Acts, by Stephen, Peter, and Paul. They are all "evangelistic" sermons, yet not one of them says anything about hell. Nothing. I'm not saying there is no hell - there is - but I'm saying this wasn't the message of apostolic preaching. How has it become the message of so much modern day preaching and evangelism? Now, Andy, I promise you I'm not going to go down a rabbit trail, but I *am* going to glance down the trail: not only do none of the apostolic sermons say anything at all about being saved from hell, in all of Paul's writings he says nothing about hell, nor does Peter, John, James or Jude - except to say that Christ went there and preached the Gospel. OK. End of glance. My point is, what has become the singular focus of the "salvation message" in much of modern Christianity simply wasn't the point at all in biblical preaching or teaching.

If salvation isn't about "not going to hell and going to heaven instead," then what *is* salvation about? To put it shortly, it is "to be conformed to the image of his Son" (Romans 8.29).

The very last thing Jesus said to his disciples before he ascended wasn't, "Go save people from hell." He said, "All authority in heaven and on earth has been given to me. Go therefore and *make disciples* of all nations, baptizing them in the name of the Father and of the Son and of the Holy Spirit, teaching them to observe all that I have commanded you. And behold, I am with you always, to the end of the age" (Matthew 28.18-20).

"Go make disciples." This was Jesus' final marching order for the Apostles, and this is what they spent their lives doing. A disciple isn't someone who has prayed the sinners prayer or made a decision for Christ. A disciple is someone who is a follower of Jesus, who is being changed by Jesus, and who is on mission with Jesus.

God's purpose for us, his will, is that we be like Jesus, that we grow into his image, that we grow in *union with God*. The Western Church calls it *sanctification*, but that word has often been read as "don't smoke, don't drink, and don't do a hundred other things that the Bible says nothing about, but about which we have rules." In other words, sanctification has too frequently been taken hostage by legalists, and the very spiritual meaning of the word - to be made holy - has been lost. The East has two other words for the process, both much more shocking but much more to the point: *deification* and *theosis*. They mean, briefly, not only being made *like* God, but also God actually working himself in us; not just into our behavior, but into our being.

Real sanctification, or theosis, or deification, doesn't happen by praying a simple prayer, making a decision, or being baptized. It happens as a process, over a long period of time (the rest of our lives, and even after). This is what "the Kingdom of God" (Jesus' favorite subject) is all about, and it ends up going so far beyond us as individuals as to literally impact and transform the whole world.

Salvation isn't being saved from hell. Although we *are* saved from hell, that isn't the point of the tale. It isn't even the first chapter or the first paragraph or even the foreword to the tale. Salvation isn't about being saved *from* hell, it is about being saved *to* God.

Victor Anselmo Boso, my friend. I am done. I pray that our exchange of words has been a good thing for you, and that it will bear much fruit in your life. Remember, my friend, "God is love."

Kenneth

❊ ❊ ❊ ❊ ❊ ❊ ❊ ❊ ❊ ❊ ❊ ❊ ❊ ❊ ❊ ❊ ❊ ❊

Dear Kenneth:

You have no idea how your corresponding with me has changed everything! I know you must be weary of my constant replies and questions by now, but I have so much to learn and so many questions to be answered. I promise I will not keep up this barrage of inquiries, but I do have one final request. Could you possibly recommend some books for my further study?

Thank you again for taking the time to dialogue with me. It has helped me immensely in my journey in Christ.

Your friend,

Andy

❋ ❋ ❋ ❋ ❋ ❋ ❋ ❋ ❋ ❋ ❋ ❋ ❋ ❋ ❋ ❋ ❋ ❋

Dear Andy:

It would be my pleasure to recommend a variety of books for you. I could probably give you fifty to read, but I will keep the list to half a dozen.

- Alfayev, Hilarion; *The Mystery of Faith*, Darton, Longman & Todd, 2002.

- Anselm of Canterbury, *The Major Works*, Oxford University Press, reissued 2008. Obviously I disagree with Anselm, but if you want to read the original thinker on the Satisfaction theory of the Atonement, this volume includes *Cur Deus Homo*.

- Carlton, Clark; *The Life: The Orthodox Doctrine of Salvation*, Regina Orthodox Press, 2000

- Myers, Kenneth; *What Christians Believe*, Mayeux Press, 2009.

- Renault, Alexander J.; *Reconsidering TULIP: A Biblical, Philosophical, and Historical Response to the Reformed Doctrine of Predestination*, self published, 2010.

•Schmemann, Alexander; *For The Life Of The World*, St. Vladimir's Seminary Press, 1973.

In addition to these, I can't encourage you enough to simply start immersing yourself in the writings of the Early Church Fathers.

Happy reading,

Ken

About the Author

Kenneth Myers was born in 1959 in Denison, Texas. The son of a pastor/missionary, he married Shirley McSorley in 1977. They have three children and four grandchildren. He is an Anglican bishop and pastors Church of the Resurrection in Sherman, Texas.

www.kennethmyers.net

Made in the USA
Charleston, SC
23 October 2015